Kathleen Kampa • Charles Vilina

Magic Time 2

Student Book

2nd Edition

OXFORD
UNIVERSITY PRESS

OXFORD
UNIVERSITY PRESS

Great Clarendon Street, Oxford, OX2 6DP, United Kingdom

Oxford University Press is a department of the University of Oxford.
It furthers the University's objective of excellence in research, scholarship,
and education by publishing worldwide. Oxford is a registered trade
mark of Oxford University Press in the UK and in certain other countries

First published in 2012
2016 2015 2014
10 9 8 7 6 5 4 3 2

ISBN: 978 0 19 401604 9 STUDENT BOOK
ISBN: 978 0 19 401603 2 STUDENT AUDIO CD
ISBN: 978 0 19 401618 6 STUDENT BOOK AND STUDENT AUDIO CD PACK

Printed in China

This book is printed on paper from certified and well-managed sources

ACKNOWLEDGEMENTS

Illustrations by: Yvette Banek, Cathy Beylon, Randy Chewning/HK Portfolio, Inc.,
Bill Colrus, Tom Hughes, Anthony Lewis/HK Portfolio, Inc., Margeaux Lucas/
HK Portfolio, Inc., Tammie Lyon, Benton Mahan, Dana Regan, Michael Reid/HK
Portfolio, Inc., George Ulrich/HK Portfolio, Inc., Jamie Smith/HK Portfolio, Inc.,
Viki Woodworth

Cover illustration by: Paul Gibbs

Musical arrangements and chant music by: William Hirtz and Steven Tolle

Original characters developed by: Amy Wummer

Our sincere gratitude to our editors and the entire Oxford University Press
family for their expert guidance in the creation and continued development
of *Magic Time*. Special thanks to our sons John and Christian, as well as to our
parents, for their love and support. Finally, to our many students, to whom
Magic Time is dedicated, thank you for making teaching the greatest profession
in the world.

Kathleen Kampa and Charles Vilina

Table of Contents

Syllabus iv

Introductions 2

Unit 1: At the Zoo 4

Unit 2: At the Aquarium 8

Unit 3: Occupations 12

Review 1 .... **16**

Talk Time 1 18

Unit 4: At the Restaurant 20

Unit 5: In the Backyard 24

Unit 6: Camping Trip 28

Review 2 .... **32**

Talk Time 2 34

Unit 7: Clock Shop 36

Unit 8: A Week at Camp Fun 40

Unit 9: World Weather 44

Review 3 .... **48**

Talk Time 3 50

Unit 10: At School 52

Unit 11: At the Park 56

Unit 12: Annie's Birthday 60

Review 4 .... **64**

Talk Time 4 66

My Picture Dictionary 68

Songs and Chants 77

Word List 83

Syllabus

Unit	Title / Topic	Word Time	Use the Words	Action Word Time	Use the Action Words	Phonics Time
1	*At the Zoo* / Animals	kangaroo gorilla penguin polar bear lion giraffe	What is it? It's a penguin.	stretch run jump swim	I can run. Me, too.	ant apple alligator baby bus butterfly
2	*At the Aquarium* / Aquarium	long fast big short slow small	It's slow. It isn't fast.	look at the turtle feed the turtle touch the starfish hold the starfish	Let's feed the turtle. Okay.	cake car cat dentist dinosaur donut
3	*Occupations* / Occupations	doctor firefighter teacher pilot vet student	She's a teacher. He's a vet.	write the word erase the word help the teacher point to the teacher	Please write the word. Sure.	elf egg elephant farmer feather fan
Review 1						
Talk Time 1 Value: Be friendly Do you like kangaroos? Yes, I do. Me, too. burgers cookies ice cream milk						
4	*At the Restaurant* / Food	pizza bread juice spaghetti salad rice	I want pizza.	pour the juice drink the juice cut the pizza eat the pizza	Drink the juice. All right.	girl goat garden horse house hen
5	*In the Backyard* / Toys	ball kite yo-yo puzzle doll jump rope	I have a kite.	push the wagon pull the wagon make the kite fly the kite	Watch me pull the wagon. Okay.	ink igloo insect jeans jar jacket
6	*Camping Trip* / Clothes	cap sweater shirt jacket skirt dress	She has a skirt. He has a sweater.	put on your cap take off your cap take out your sweater put away your sweater	Take out your sweater quickly.	ketchup key king lizard leaf lemon mouse moon monkey
Review 2						
Talk Time 2 Value: Be kind You can use my jump rope. Really? Thank you! You're welcome. umbrella camera hula hoop skateboard						

Unit	Title / Topic	Word Time	Use the Words	Action Word Time	Use the Action Words	Phonics Time
7	*Clock Shop* / Time	one o'clock – twelve o'clock	What time is it? It's two o'clock.	pick up the clock put down the clock open the door close the door	Put down the clock slowly.	**n**umbers **n**est **n**ecklace **o**x **o**ffice **o**ctopus
8	*A Week at Camp Fun* / Days of the Week	Sunday Monday Tuesday Wednesday Thursday Friday Saturday	What day is it? Today is Sunday.	plant a tree climb a tree draw a picture paint a picture	Draw a picture with me. Sure.	**p**uppy **p**opcorn **p**arrot **q**ueen **q**uilt **q**uestion mark
9	*World Weather* / Weather	sunny hot windy cloudy cold rainy	How's the weather? It's windy.	get on the train get off the train get in the car get out of the car	Let's get off the train. All right.	**r**ooster **r**ainbow **r**abbit **s**eal **s**ailboat **s**un

Review 3

Talk Time 3 Value: Don't be late   We're late.   Please get on the train.   Okay, Mom.
brush your teeth   wash your face   get dressed   pack your bag

Unit	Title / Topic	Word Time	Use the Words	Action Word Time	Use the Action Words	Phonics Time
10	*At School* / School Activities	sing songs write stories read books color pictures do jumping jacks hold hands	We read books at school	raise your hand put down your hand talk to your friend listen to your friend	Please raise your hand. Okay.	**t**iger **t**able **t**elephone **u**mbrella **u**mpire **u**pside down
11	*At the Park* / Sports and Hobbies	play basketball play soccer play cards play chess play the violin play the piano	Can you play soccer? Yes, I can. No, I can't.	bounce the basketball catch the basketball kick the soccer ball throw the soccer ball	I can bounce the basketball. Great!	**v**ase **v**iolin **v**est **w**orm **w**atermelon **w**indow
12	*Annie's Birthday* / Rooms of a House	bedroom bathroom yard living room dining room kitchen	Where are you? I'm in the kitchen.	wash the dishes dry the dishes turn on the light turn off the light	Turn off the light, please. All right.	fox zebra box zipper six zero yarn yo-yo yellow

Review 4

Talk Time 4 Value: Be prepared   I'm ready to play the piano.   Good! Let's get started.   Sure.
bake cookies   clean the house   study English   rake the leaves

Introductions

A. 🎵 CD1 1 Listen and repeat.

B. 🎵 CD1 2 Listen and point below. 👇

1.

Annie

2.

Ted

3.

Digger

4.

Dot

5.

Kelly

6. 7. 8. 9. 10.

Pat Kumi Joe Jane Chris

Word Time

A. CD1 4 Look and listen.

kangaroo

gorilla

penguin

polar bear

lion

giraffe

B. CD1 5 Listen, point, and repeat.

C. CD1 6 Listen and point below. Then chant. 🎵 2

D. CD1 7 Listen and write the number. ✏️

Use the Words

A. 🔊 CD1 8 Listen and repeat.

> What is it?

> It's a penguin.

B. 🔊 CD1 9 Listen and point below. 👇

C. 🔊 CD1 10 Listen and point. Then sing along. 🎵🎶 3

Action Word Time

A. 🔊 CD1 11 Look and listen.

B. 🔊 CD1 12 Listen, point, and repeat.

stretch

run

jump

swim

C. 🔊 CD1 13 Listen and repeat.

I can run.

Me, too.

D. 🔊 CD1 14 Listen and point below. 👇

E. 🔊 CD1 15 Listen and point. Then sing along. 🎵🎵 4

Phonics Time

A. Make the shape of each letter.

A   a   B   b

B. CD1 16 Listen and point.

ant   alligator   apple   baby   butterfly   bus

C. CD1 17 Listen and point. Then sing along. ♫ 5

Word Time

A. 🎵 CD1 18 Look and listen.

B. 🎵 CD1 19 Listen, point, and repeat.

long

fast

big

short

slow

small

C. 🎵 CD1 20 Listen and point below. Then chant. 👇 🎵🎵 6

D. 🎵 CD1 21 Listen and write the number. ✏️

Use the Words

A. CD1 22 Listen and repeat.

> It's slow. It isn't fast.

B. CD1 23 Listen and point below.

C. CD1 24 Listen and point. Then sing along.

Action Word Time

A. CD1 25 Look and listen.

B. CD1 26 Listen, point, and repeat.

look at the turtle   feed the turtle   touch the starfish   hold the starfish

C. CD1 27 Listen and repeat.

Let's feed the turtle.

Okay.

D. CD1 28 Listen and point below.

E. CD1 29 Listen and point. Then sing along. 8

Phonics Time

A. Make the shape of each letter.

C   c   D   d

B. (CD1 30) Listen and point.

cake   car

cat

dentist   dinosaur

donut

C. (CD1 31) Listen and point. Then sing along. ♪♪ 9

Word Time

A. 🎧 CD1 32 Look and listen.

doctor

firefighter

pilot

vet

B. 🎧 CD1 33 Listen, point, and repeat.

teacher

student

C. 🎧 CD1 34 Listen and point below. Then chant. 👇 🎵 10

D. 🎧 CD1 35 Listen and write the number. ✏️

Use the Words

A. 🎧 CD1 36 Listen and repeat.

She's a teacher.

He's a vet.

B. 🎧 CD1 37 Listen and point below. 👇

C. 🎧 CD1 38 Listen and point. Then sing along. 🎵🎵 11

Action Word Time

A. CD1 39 Look and listen.

doctor

write the word

firefighter fighter

erase the word

B. CD1 40 Listen, point, and repeat.

help the teacher

point to the teacher

C. CD1 41 Listen and repeat.

Please write the word.

doctor

Sure.

D. CD1 42 Listen and point below.

E. CD1 43 Listen and point. Then sing along. 12

Phonics Time

A. Make the shape of each letter.

E   e   F   f

B. CD1 44 Listen and point.

elf   elephant   egg   farmer   fan   feather

C. CD1 45 Listen and point. Then sing along. ♪♪ 13

A. CD1 46 Listen and match. ✏️

1. •   2. •   3. •   4. •   5. •   6. •

B. CD1 47 Listen and write the number. ✏️

C. Trace the letters. Then circle and connect. ✏️

Aa   Bb   Cc   Dd   Ee   Ff

A. 🎧 CD1 48 Listen and connect. ✏️

1. •

2. •

3. •

4. •

B. 🎧 CD1 49 Listen and write the number. ✏️

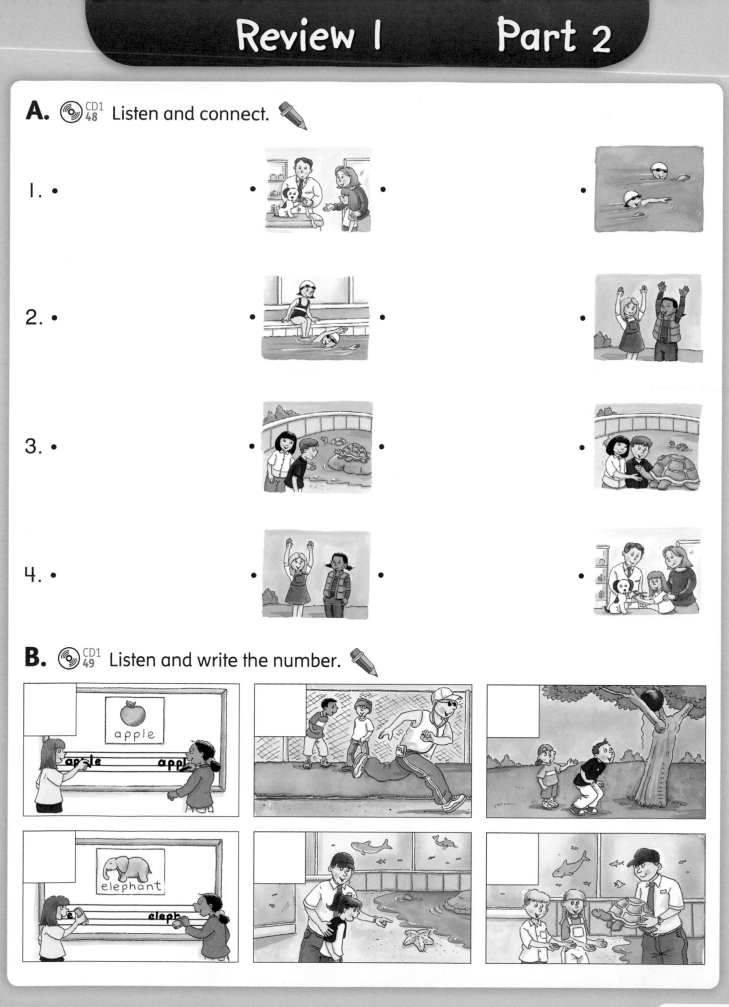

A. 🔘 CD1 50 Listen and point below. 👇

B. 🔘 CD1 51 Listen, point, and repeat.

Be friendly

1. Do you like kangaroos?

2. Yes, I do.

3. Me, too.

C. 🔘 CD1 52 Listen and practice with a friend.

 penguin

 giraffe

 lion

 kangaroo

gorilla

 polar bear

Do you like penguins?

Yes, I do.

Me, too.

A. 🔊 CD1 53 Listen and repeat.

burgers   cookies   ice cream   milk

B. 🔊 CD1 54 Listen and write the number. ✏️

C. 🔊 CD1 55 Listen and point. Then sing along. 🎵🎵 14

Word Time

A. CD1 56 Look and listen.

B. CD1 57 Listen, point, and repeat.

pizza

bread

juice

spaghetti

salad

rice

C. CD1 58 Listen and point below. Then chant. 15

D. CD1 59 Listen and write the number.

Use the Words

A. 🎵 CD1 60 Listen and repeat.

I want pizza.

B. 🎵 CD1 61 Listen and point below. 👇

C. 🎵 CD1 62 Listen and point. Then sing along. 🎵 16

Action Word Time

A. 🔊 CD1 63 Look and listen.

pour the juice   drink the juice

B. 🔊 CD1 64 Listen, point, and repeat.

cut the pizza   eat the pizza

C. 🔊 CD1 65 Listen and repeat.

Drink the juice.

All right.

D. 🔊 CD1 66 Listen and point below. 👇

E. 🔊 CD1 67 Listen and point. Then sing along. 🎵🎵 17

Phonics Time

A. Make the shape of each letter.

G g H h

B. CD1 68 Listen and point.

girl   goat

garden

horse   hen   house

C. CD1 69 Listen and point. Then sing along. ♫ 18

Word Time

A. 🔊 CD2 1 Look and listen.   **B.** 🔊 CD2 2 Listen, point, and repeat.

ball   kite   yo-yo

puzzle   doll   jump rope

C. 🔊 CD2 3 Listen and point below. Then chant. 🎵 19

D. 🔊 CD2 4 Listen and write the number. ✏️

Use the Words

A. 🔘 CD2 5 Listen and repeat.

> I have a kite.

B. 🔘 CD2 6 Listen and point below. 👇

C. 🔘 CD2 7 Listen and point. Then sing along. 🎵 20

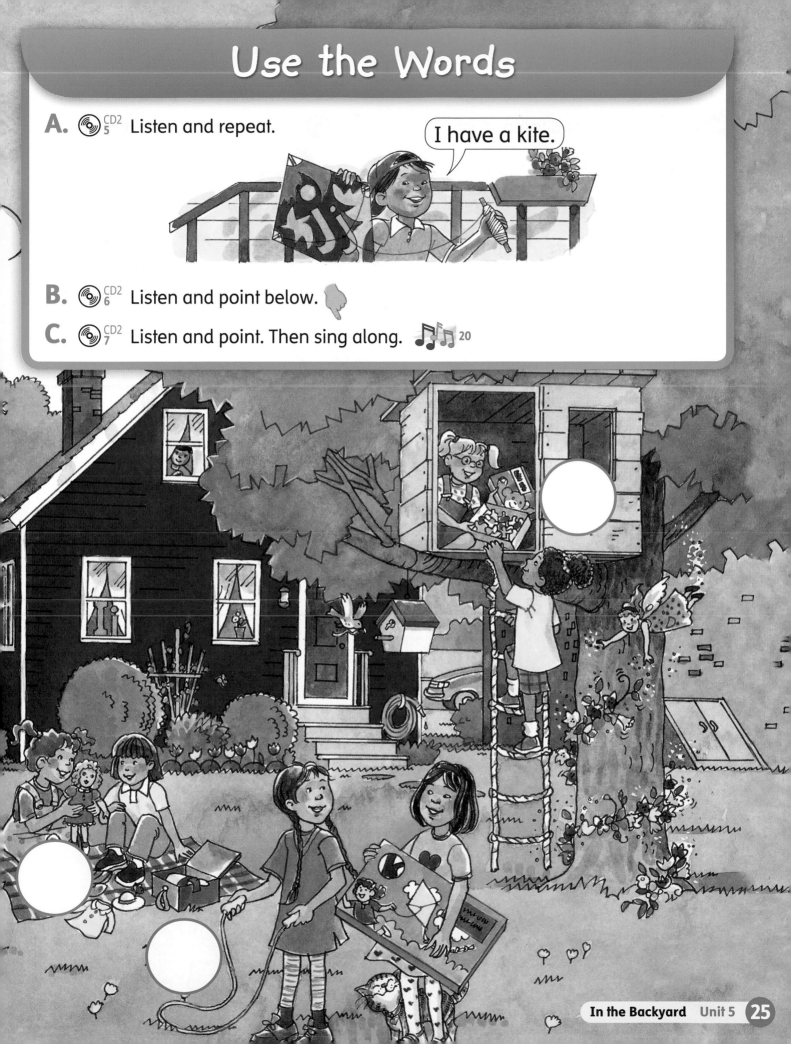

Action Word Time

A. (CD2 8) Look and listen.

push the wagon   pull the wagon

B. (CD2 9) Listen, point, and repeat.

make the kite   fly the kite

C. (CD2 10) Listen and repeat.

Watch me pull the wagon.

Okay.

D. (CD2 11) Listen and point below.

E. (CD2 12) Listen and point. Then sing along. ♪♫ 21

Phonics Time

A. Make the shape of each letter.

I   i   J   j

B. 🎵 CD2 13 Listen and point. 👇

ink   igloo   jeans   jar

insect   jacket

C. 🎵 CD2 14 Listen and point. Then sing along. 🎵🎵 22

Word Time

A. CD2 15 Look and listen.

cap

sweater

B. CD2 16 Listen, point, and repeat.

shirt

jacket

skirt

dress

C. CD2 17 Listen and point below. Then chant. ♪♪ 23

D. CD2 18 Listen and write the number. ✏️

Kk

Use the Words

A.  Listen and repeat.

"She has a skirt."

"He has a sweater."

B. 🔊 CD2 20 Listen and point below. 👇

C. 🔊 CD2 21 Listen and point. Then sing along. 🎵 24

Action Word Time

A. CD2 22 Look and listen.

put on
your cap

take off
your cap

B. CD2 23 Listen, point, and repeat.

take out
your sweater

put away
your sweater

C. CD2 24 Listen and repeat.

Take out your sweater quickly.

D. CD2 25 Listen and point below.

E. CD2 26 Listen and point. Then sing along. 25

Phonics Time

A. Make the shape of each letter.

K   k   L   I   M   m

B. 🔊 CD2 27 Listen and point. 👆

ketchup   key
king

lizard   leaf
lemon

mouse   moon
monkey

C. 🔊 CD2 28 Listen and point. Then sing along. 🎵 26

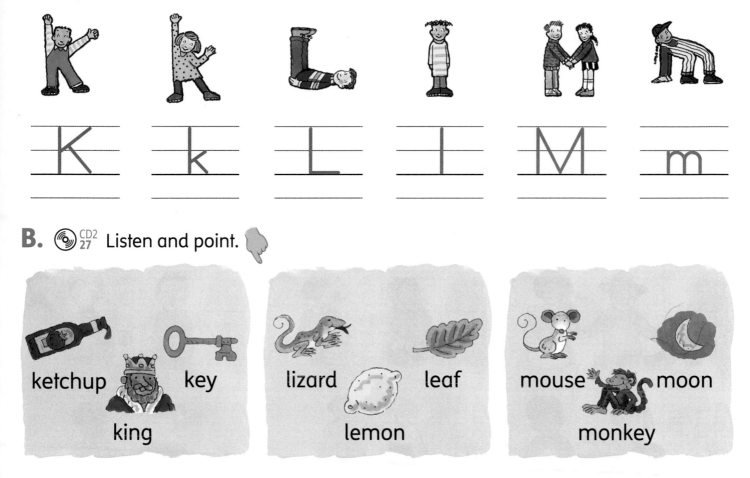

A. CD2 29 Listen and match. ✏️

1. • 2. • 3. • 4. • 5. • 6. •

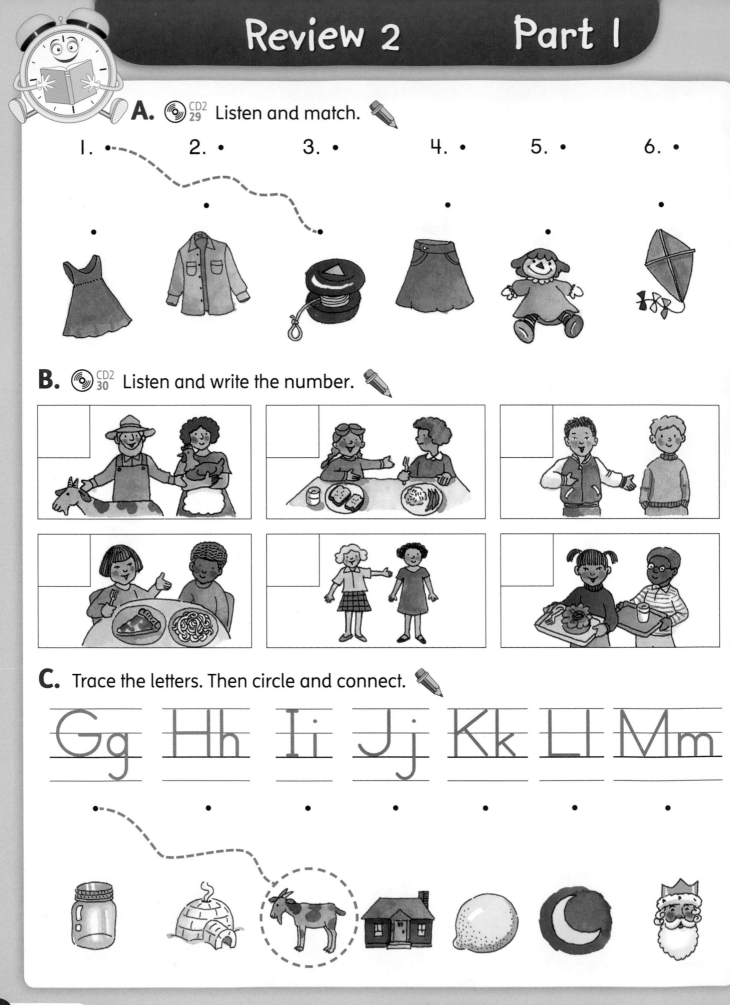

B. CD2 30 Listen and write the number. ✏️

C. Trace the letters. Then circle and connect. ✏️

Gg Hh Ii Jj Kk Ll Mm

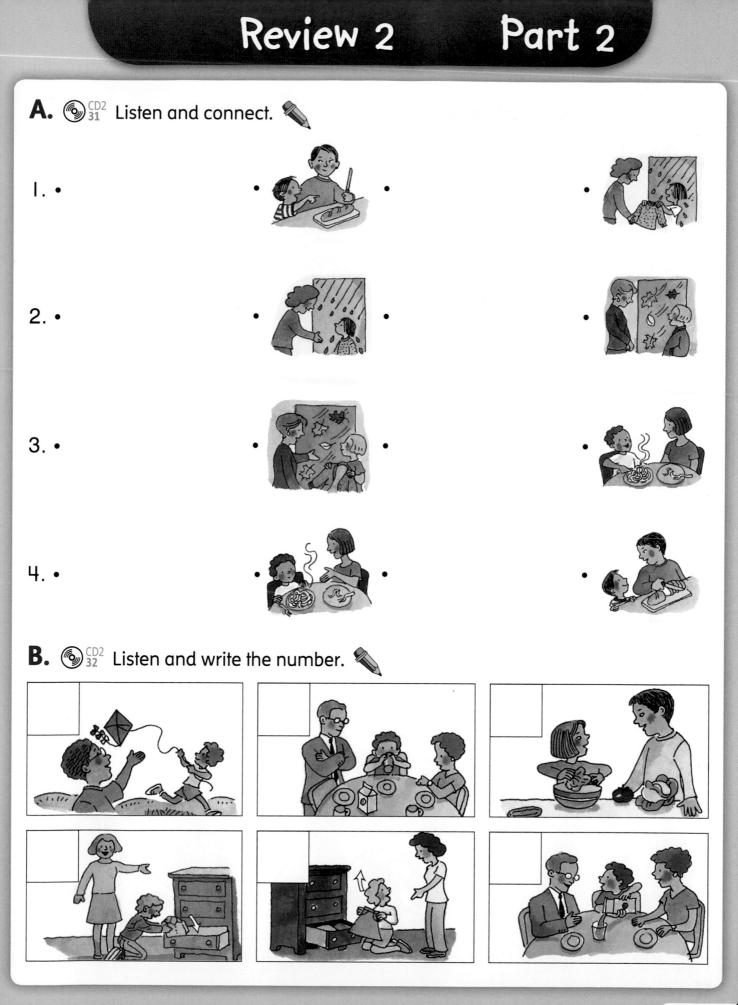

A. 🎧 CD2 31 Listen and connect. ✏️

1. •

2. •

3. •

4. •

B. 🎧 CD2 32 Listen and write the number. ✏️

A. CD2 33   Listen and point below.

B. CD2 34   Listen, point, and repeat.

C. CD2 35   Listen and practice with a friend.

A. 🎧 CD2 36 Listen and repeat.

umbrella   camera   hula hoop   skateboard

B. 🎧 CD2 37 Listen and write the number. ✏️

C. 🎧 CD2 38 Listen and point. Then sing along. 🎵 27

Word Time

A. 🔊 CD2 39 Look and listen.

1:00 one o'clock	**2:00** two o'clock
5:00 five o'clock	**6:00** six o'clock
9:00 nine o'clock	**10:00** ten o'clock

B. 🔊 CD2 40 Listen, point, and repeat.

3:00 three o'clock	**4:00** four o'clock
7:00 seven o'clock	**8:00** eight o'clock
11:00 eleven o'clock	**12:00** twelve o'clock

C. 🔊 CD2 41 Listen and point below. Then chant. 👇 🎵🎵 28

D. 🔊 CD2 42 Listen and write the number. ✏️

Use the Words

A. CD2 43 Listen and repeat.

What time is it?

It's two o'clock.

B. CD2 44 Listen and point below.

C. CD2 45 Listen and point. Then sing along. 29

Action Word Time

A. CD2 46 Look and listen.

pick up
the clock

put down
the clock

B. CD2 47 Listen, point, and repeat.

open
the door

close
the door

C. CD2 48 Listen and repeat.

Put down the clock slowly.

D. CD2 49 Listen and point below.

E. CD2 50 Listen and point. Then sing along. 30

Phonics Time

A. Make the shape of each letter.

N   n   O   o

B. CD2 51 Listen and point.

numbers

necklace

nest

ox

octopus

office

C. CD2 52 Listen and point. Then sing along. ♪♫ 31

Word Time

A. 🔘 CD2 53 Look and listen. **B.** 🔘 CD2 54 Listen, point, and repeat.

Sunday	Monday	Tuesday	Wednesday	Thursday	Friday	Saturday

Sunday   Monday   Tuesday   Wednesday   Thursday   Friday   Saturday

C. 🔘 CD2 55 Listen and point below. Then chant. 👇 🎵🎵 32

D. 🔘 CD2 56 Listen and write the number. ✏️

Sunday

Monday

Tuesday

Use the Words

A. CD2 57 Listen and repeat.

B. CD2 58 Listen and point below.

C. CD2 59 Listen and point. Then sing along. 33

Action Word Time

A. CD2 60 Look and listen.

plant a tree   climb a tree

B. CD2 61 Listen, point, and repeat.

draw a picture   paint a picture

C. CD2 62 Listen and repeat.

Draw a picture with me.

Sure.

D. CD2 63 Listen and point below.

E. CD2 64 Listen and point. Then sing along. ♪♫ 34

Camp Fun

Phonics Time

A. Make the shape of each letter.

P p Q q

B. CD2 65 Listen and point.

puppy   parrot   popcorn

queen   question mark   quilt

C. CD2 66 Listen and point. Then sing along. ♪♫ 35

Word Time

9

A. 🎧 CD3 1 Look and listen.

sunny

cloudy

hot

cold

B. 🎧 CD3 2 Listen, point, and repeat.

windy

rainy

C. 🎧 CD3 3 Listen and point below. Then chant. 👇 🎵🎵 36

D. 🎧 CD3 4 Listen and write the number. ✏️

Ss

Use the Words

A. 🔊 CD3 5 Listen and repeat.

> How's the weather?

> It's windy.

B. 🔊 CD3 6 Listen and point below. 👇

C. 🔊 CD3 7 Listen and point. Then sing along. 🎵 37

Action Word Time

A. 🔊 CD3 8 Look and listen.

get on the train　　get off the train

B. 🔊 CD3 9 Listen, point, and repeat.

get in the car　　get out of the car

C. 🔊 CD3 10 Listen and repeat.

Let's get off the train.

All right.

D. 🔊 CD3 11 Listen and point below. 👉

E. 🔊 CD3 12 Listen and point. Then sing along. 🎵 38

Phonics Time

A. Make the shape of each letter.

R   r   S   s

B. CD3 13 Listen and point. 👇

rooster   rabbit   rainbow   seal   sun   sailboat

C. CD3 14 Listen and point. Then sing along. ♫♪ 39

A. 🔊 CD3 15 Listen and match. ✏️

1. •   2. •   3. •   4. •   5. •   6. •

B. 🔊 CD3 16 Listen and write the number. ✏️

C. Trace the letters. Then circle and connect. ✏️

Nn   Oo   Pp   Qq   Rr   Ss

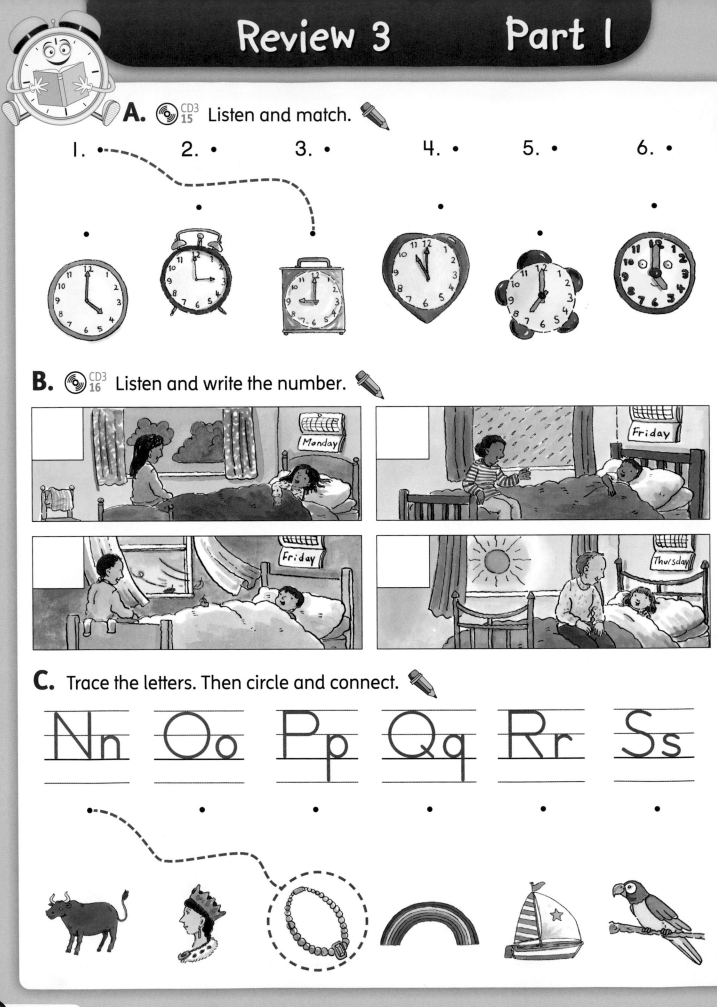

A. CD3 17 Listen and connect. ✏️

1. •

2. •

3. •

4. •

B. CD3 18 Listen and write the number. ✏️

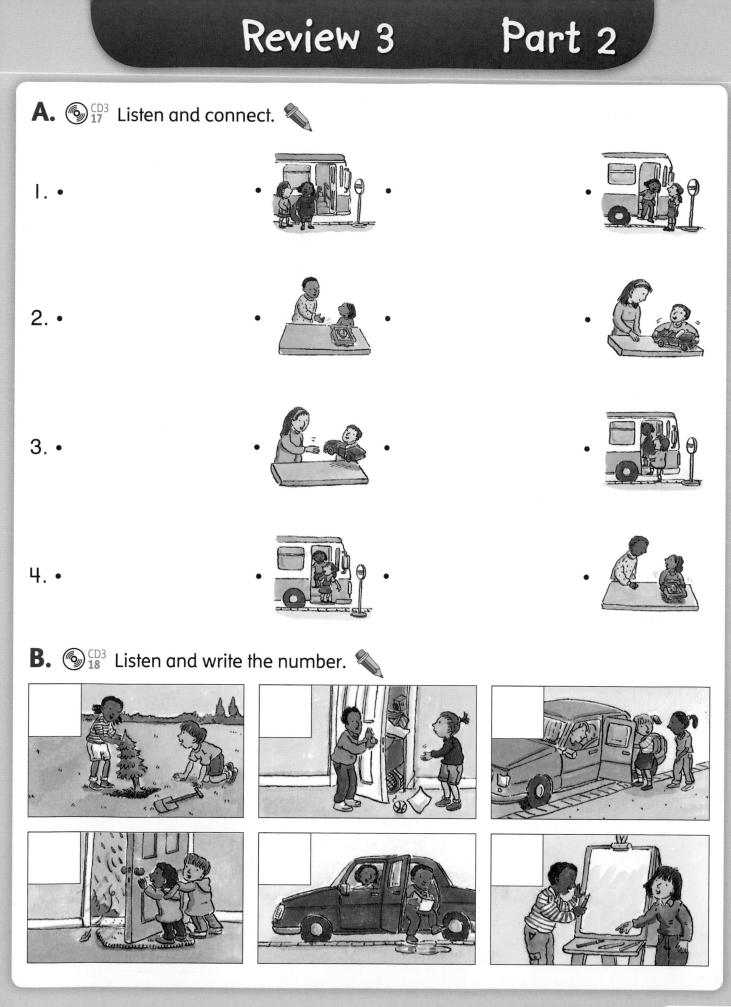

A. CD3 19 Listen and point below.

B. CD3 20 Listen, point, and repeat.

Don't be late

1. We're late.

2. Please get on the train.

3. Okay, Mom.

C. CD3 21 Listen and practice with a friend.

get on the train

get off the train

get in the car

get out of the car

We're late.

Please get in the car.

Okay, Dad.

A. 🔊 CD3 22 Listen and repeat.

brush your teeth	wash your face	get dressed	pack your bag

B. 🔊 CD3 23 Listen and write the number. ✏️

8:30 AM

7:15

C. 🔊 CD3 24 Listen and point. Then sing along. 🎵🎵 40

Word Time

10

A. CD3 25 Look and listen.

sing songs

write stories

read books

color pictures

do jumping jacks

hold hands

B. CD3 26 Listen, point, and repeat.

C. CD3 27 Listen and point below. Then chant. 🎵🎶 41

D. CD3 28 Listen and write the number. ✏️

Use the Words

A. CD3 29 Listen and repeat.

We read books at school.

B. CD3 30 Listen and point below. 👇

C. CD3 31 Listen and point. Then sing along. 🎵🎵 42

Action Word Time

A. (CD3 32) Look and listen.

raise
your hand

put down
your hand

B. (CD3 33) Listen, point, and repeat.

talk to
your friend

listen to
your friend

C. (CD3 34) Listen and repeat.

Please raise your hand.

Okay.

D. (CD3 35) Listen and point below.

E. (CD3 36) Listen and point. Then sing along. 43

Phonics Time

A. Make the shape of each letter.

B. 🔘 CD3 37 Listen and point. 👇

tiger   telephone   table

umbrella   upside down   umpire

C. 🔘 CD3 38 Listen and point. Then sing along. 🎵 44

Word Time

A. CD3 39 Look and listen.

B. CD3 40 Listen, point, and repeat.

play basketball

play soccer

play cards

play chess

play the violin

play the piano

C. CD3 41 Listen and point below. Then chant. 🎵 45

D. CD3 42 Listen and write the number. ✏️

Use the Words

A. CD3 43 Listen and repeat.

Can you play soccer?

No, I can't.

Yes, I can.

B. CD3 44 Listen and point below.

C. CD3 45 Listen and point. Then sing along. 46

Action Word Time

A. 🔘 CD3 46 Look and listen.

bounce the
basketball

catch the
basketball

B. 🔘 CD3 47 Listen, point, and repeat.

kick the
soccer ball

throw the
soccer ball

C. 🔘 CD3 48 Listen and repeat.

I can bounce the basketball.

Great!

D. 🔘 CD3 49 Listen and point below.

E. 🔘 CD3 50 Listen and point. Then sing along. 🎵🎵 47

Phonics Time

A. Make the shape of each letter.

V V W W

B. 🔊 CD3 51 Listen and point. 👇

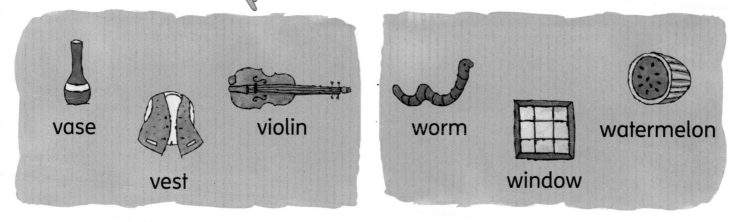

vase

vest

violin

worm

window

watermelon

C. 🔊 CD3 52 Listen and point. Then sing along. 🎵 48

Word Time

A. CD3 53 Look and listen.

bedroom

bathroom

yard

living room

dining room

kitchen

B. CD3 54 Listen, point, and repeat.

C. CD3 55 Listen and point below. Then chant. 🎵🎵 49

D. CD3 56 Listen and write the number. ✏️

Use the Words

A. 🔊 CD3 57 Listen and repeat.

Where are you?

I'm in the kitchen.

B. 🔊 CD3 58 Listen and point below. 👇

C. 🔊 CD3 59 Listen and point. Then sing along. 🎵 50

Action Word Time

A. 🔘 CD3 60 Look and listen.

wash the dishes   dry the dishes

B. 🔘 CD3 61 Listen, point, and repeat.

turn on the light   turn off the light

C. 🔘 CD3 62 Listen and repeat.

Turn off the light, please.

All right.

D. 🔘 CD3 63 Listen and point below. 👇

E. 🔘 CD3 64 Listen and point. Then sing along. 🎵🎵 51

Phonics Time

A. Make the shape of each letter.

B. CD3 65 Listen and point. 👇

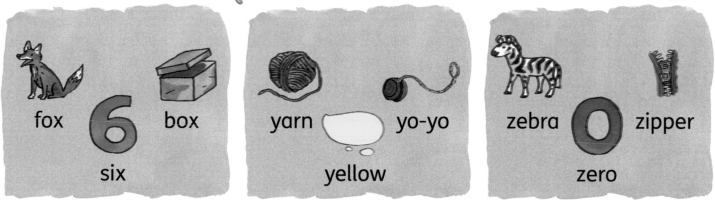

fox	**6**	box
	six	

yarn yo-yo

yellow

zebra **0** zipper

zero

C. CD3 66 Listen and point. Then sing along. 🎵 52

A. CD3 67 Listen and match.

1. •   2. •   3. •   4. •   5. •   6. •

B. CD3 68 Listen and write the number.

C. Trace the letters. Then circle and connect.

Tt Uu Vv Ww Xx Yy Zz

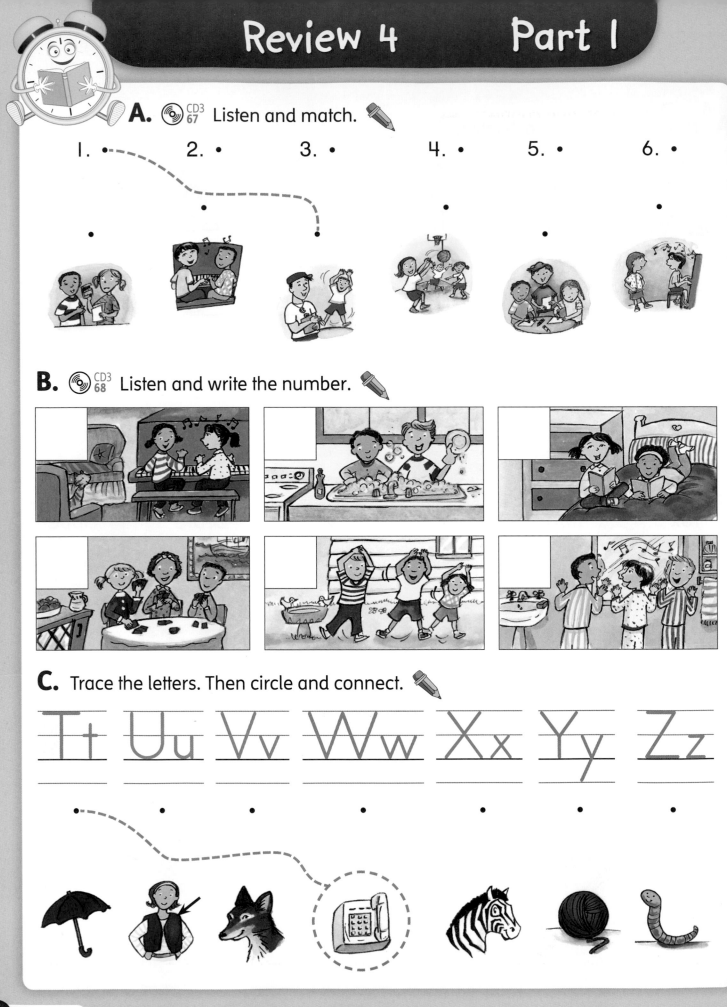

A. 🎧 CD3 69 Listen and connect. ✏️

1. •

2. •

3. •

4. •

B. 🎧 CD3 70 Listen and write the number. ✏️

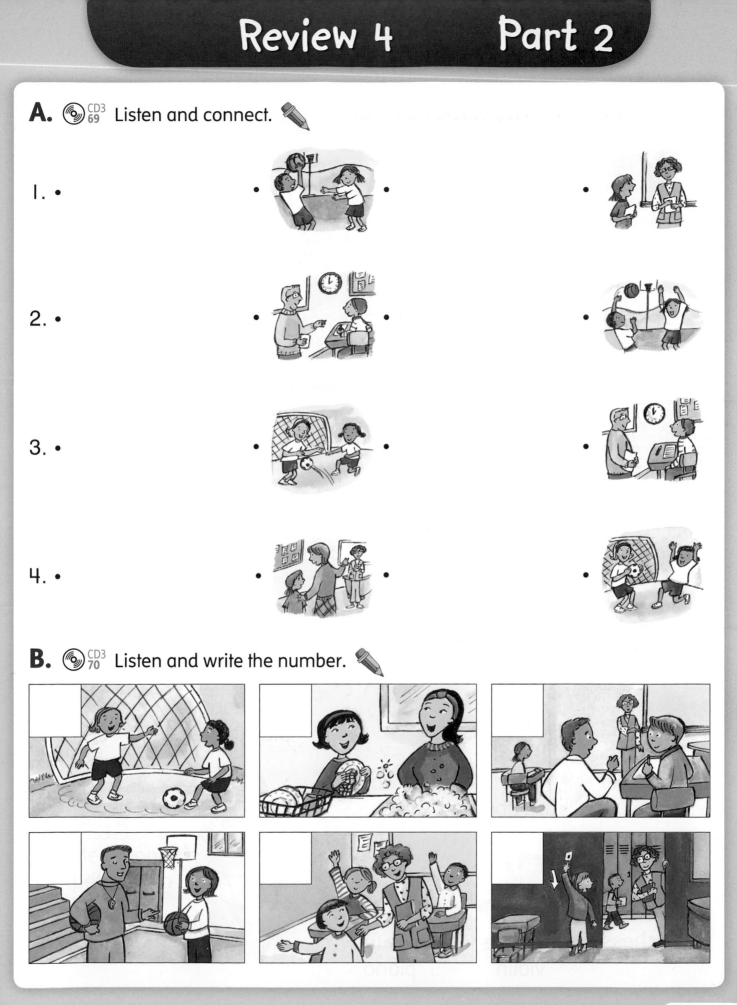

A. 🔘 CD3 71 Listen and point below. 👆

B. 🔘 CD3 72 Listen, point, and repeat.

Be prepared

1. I'm ready to play the piano.

2. Good! Let's get started.

3. Okay.

C. 🔘 CD3 73 Listen and practice with a friend.

play soccer

play basketball

play cards

play chess

play the violin

play the piano

I'm ready to play soccer.

Good! Let's get started.

Okay.

A. CD3 74 Listen and repeat.

bake cookies	clean the house	study English	rake the leaves

B. CD3 75 Listen and write the number.

C. CD3 76 Listen and point. Then sing along. 53

My Picture Dictionary

Check (✔) the words you know.

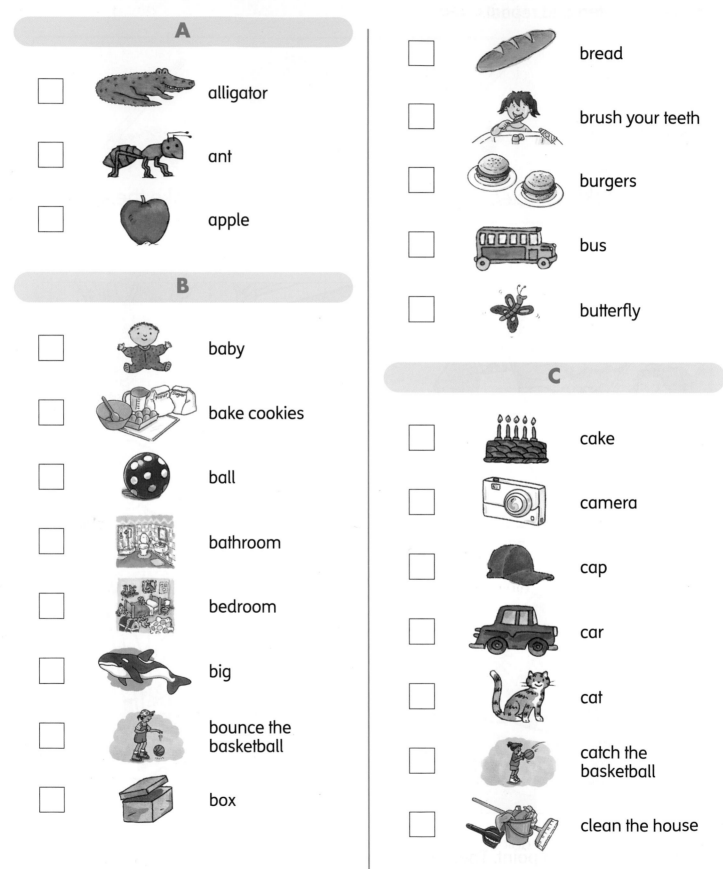

A

- [ ] alligator
- [ ] ant
- [ ] apple

B

- [ ] baby
- [ ] bake cookies
- [ ] ball
- [ ] bathroom
- [ ] bedroom
- [ ] big
- [ ] bounce the basketball
- [ ] box

- [ ] bread
- [ ] brush your teeth
- [ ] burgers
- [ ] bus
- [ ] butterfly

C

- [ ] cake
- [ ] camera
- [ ] cap
- [ ] car
- [ ] cat
- [ ] catch the basketball
- [ ] clean the house

- [ ]  climb a tree
- [ ] close the door
- [ ] cloudy
- [ ] cold
- [ ] color pictures
- [ ] cookies
- [ ] cut the pizza

D

- [ ] dentist
- [ ] dining room
- [ ] dinosaur
- [ ] do jumping jacks
- [ ] doctor
- [ ] doll

- [ ] donut
- [ ] draw a picture
- [ ] dress
- [ ] drink the juice
- [ ] dry the dishes

E

- [ ] eat the pizza
- [ ] egg
- [ ] eight o'clock
- [ ] elephant
- [ ] eleven o'clock
- [ ] elf
- [ ] erase the word

F

- [ ] fan
- [ ] farmer
- [ ] fast
- [ ] feather
- [ ] feed the turtle
- [ ] firefighter
- [ ] five o'clock
- [ ] fly the kite
- [ ] four o'clock
- [ ] fox
- [ ] Friday

G

- [ ] garden
- [ ] get dressed
- [ ] get in the car
- [ ] get off the train
- [ ] get on the train
- [ ] get out of the car
- [ ] giraffe
- [ ] girl
- [ ] goat
- [ ] gorilla

H

- [ ] help the teacher
- [ ] hen
- [ ] hold hands
- [ ] hold the starfish

- ☐ horse
- ☐ hot
- ☐ house
- ☐ hula hoop

I

- ☐ ice cream
- ☐ igloo
- ☐ ink
- ☐ insect

J

- ☐ jacket
- ☐ jar
- ☐ jeans
- ☐ juice

- ☐ jump
- ☐ jump rope

K

- ☐ kangaroo
- ☐ ketchup
- ☐ key
- ☐ kick the soccer ball
- ☐ king
- ☐ kitchen
- ☐ kite

L

- ☐ leaf
- ☐ lemon
- ☐ lion

- [ ] listen to your friend
- [ ] living room
- [ ] lizard
- [ ] long
- [ ] look at the turtle

M

- [ ] make the kite
- [ ] milk
- [ ] Monday
- [ ] monkey
- [ ] moon
- [ ] mouse

N

- [ ] necklace

- [ ] nest
- [ ] nine o'clock
- [ ] numbers

O

- [ ] octopus
- [ ] office
- [ ] one o'clock
- [ ] open the door
- [ ] ox

P

- [ ] pack your bag
- [ ] paint a picture
- [ ] parrot
- [ ] penguin

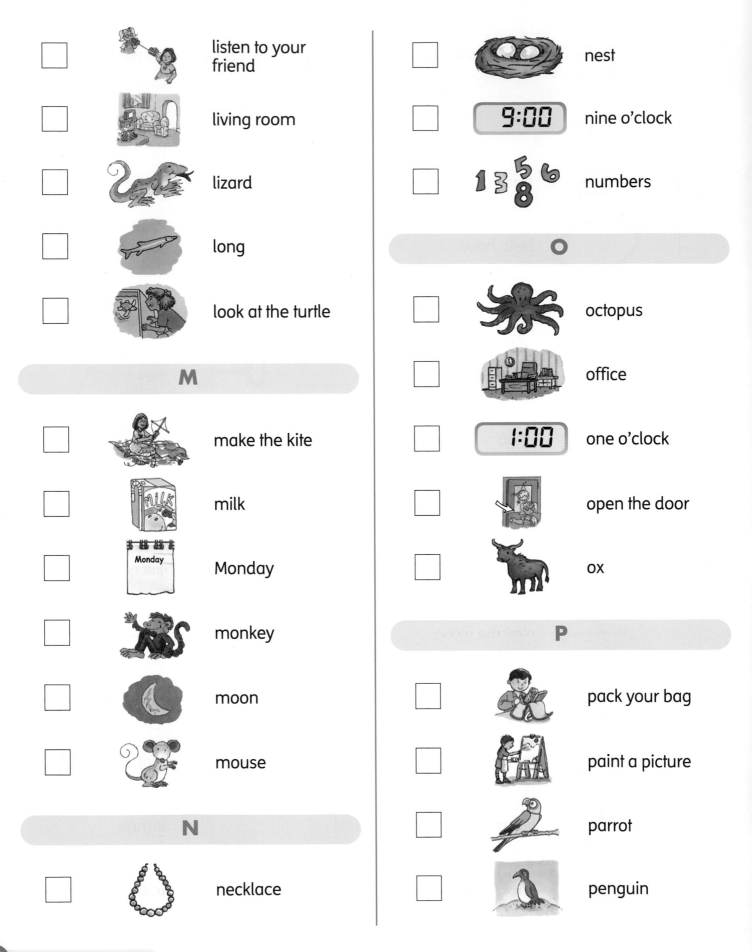

☐	pick up the clock
☐	pilot
☐	pizza
☐	plant a tree
☐	play basketball
☐	play cards
☐	play chess
☐	play soccer
☐	play the piano
☐	play the violin
☐	point to the teacher
☐	polar bear
☐	popcorn
☐	pour the juice

☐	pull the wagon
☐	puppy
☐	push the wagon
☐	put away your sweater
☐	put down the clock
☐	put down your hand
☐	put on your cap
☐	puzzle

Q

☐	queen
☐	question mark
☐	quilt

R

☐	rabbit

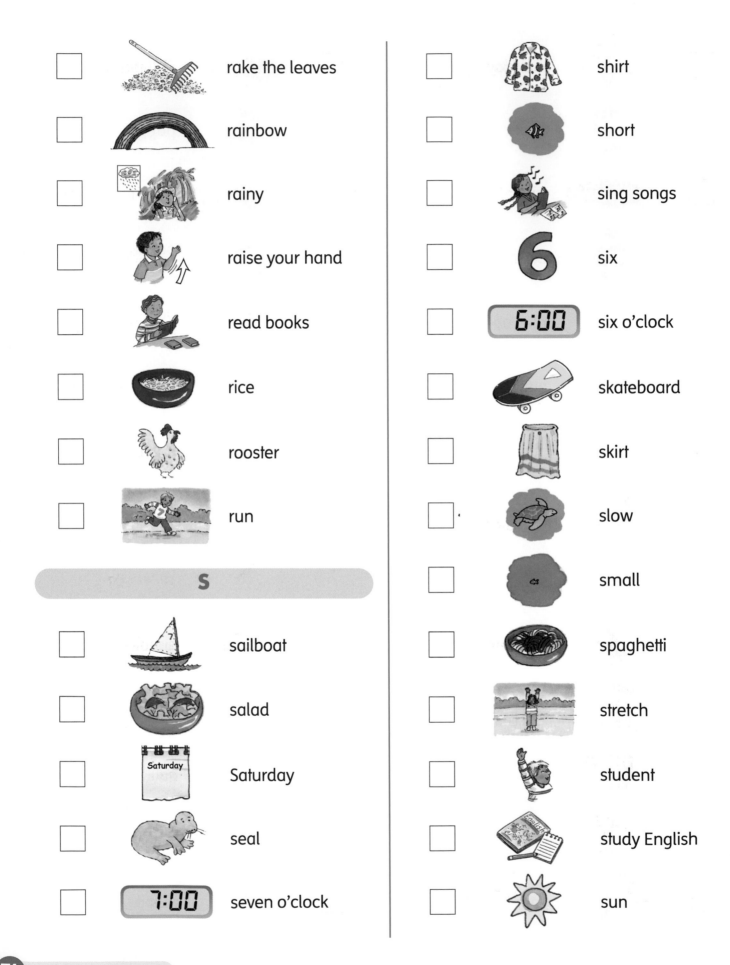

- [ ] rake the leaves
- [ ] rainbow
- [ ] rainy
- [ ] raise your hand
- [ ] read books
- [ ] rice
- [ ] rooster
- [ ] run

S

- [ ] sailboat
- [ ] salad
- [ ] Saturday
- [ ] seal
- [ ] seven o'clock

- [ ] shirt
- [ ] short
- [ ] sing songs
- [ ] six
- [ ] six o'clock
- [ ] skateboard
- [ ] skirt
- [ ] slow
- [ ] small
- [ ] spaghetti
- [ ] stretch
- [ ] student
- [ ] study English
- [ ] sun

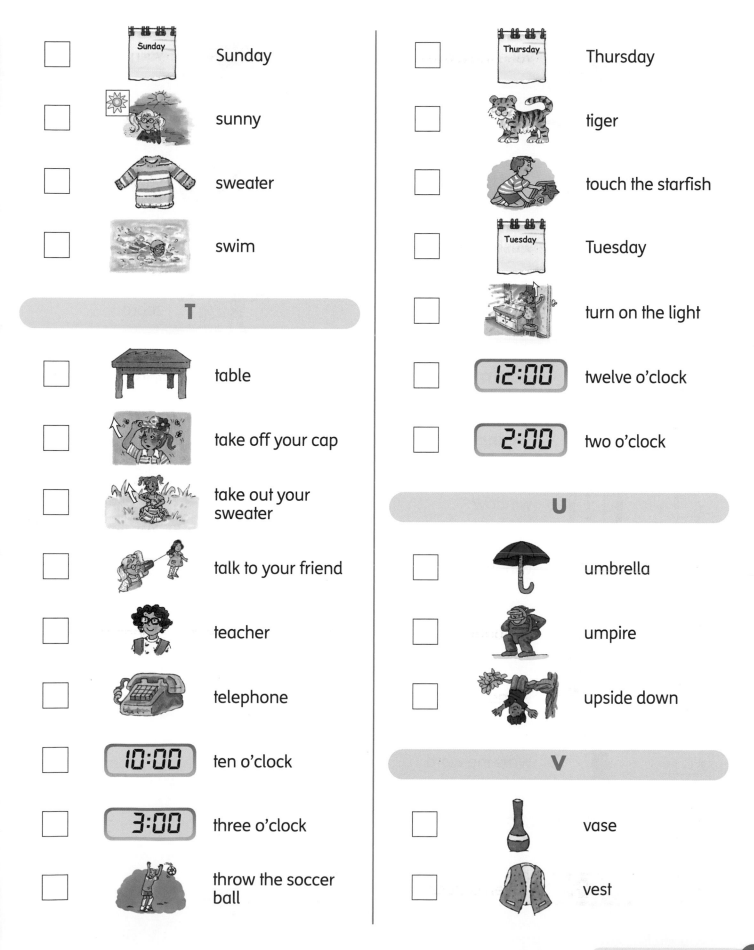

- [ ] Sunday
- [ ] sunny
- [ ] sweater
- [ ] swim

T

- [ ] table
- [ ] take off your cap
- [ ] take out your sweater
- [ ] talk to your friend
- [ ] teacher
- [ ] telephone
- [ ] ten o'clock
- [ ] three o'clock
- [ ] throw the soccer ball

- [ ] Thursday
- [ ] tiger
- [ ] touch the starfish
- [ ] Tuesday
- [ ] turn on the light
- [ ] twelve o'clock
- [ ] two o'clock

U

- [ ] umbrella
- [ ] umpire
- [ ] upside down

V

- [ ] vase
- [ ] vest

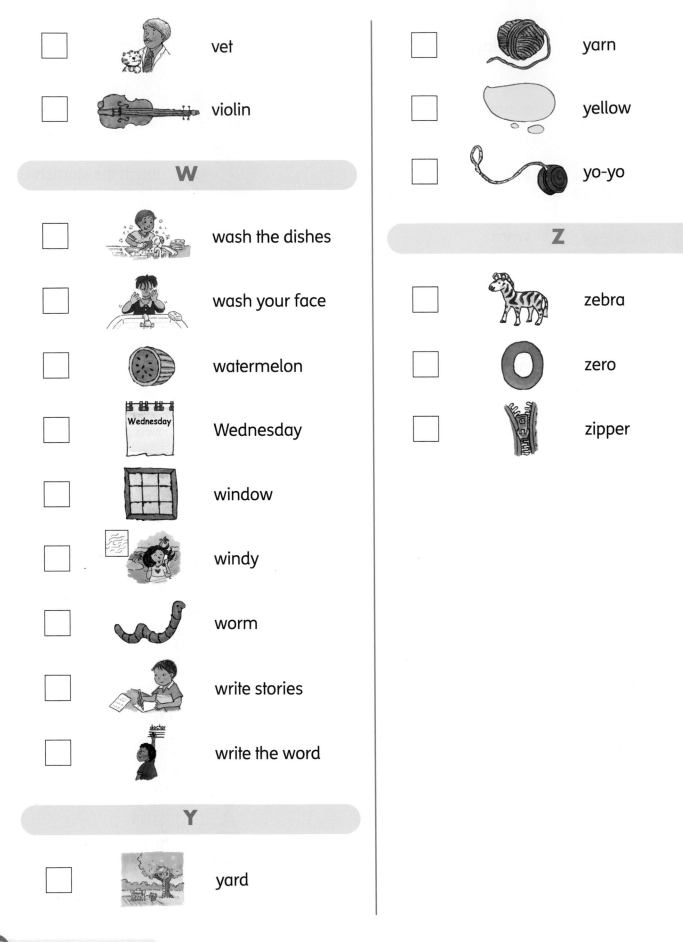

☐ vet

☐ violin

W

☐ wash the dishes

☐ wash your face

☐ watermelon

☐ Wednesday

☐ window

☐ windy

☐ worm

☐ write stories

☐ write the word

Y

☐ yard

☐ yarn

☐ yellow

☐ yo-yo

Z

☐ zebra

☐ zero

☐ zipper

Songs and Chants

Introductions

The Hello Song

Hello! I'm Annie. Hello, hello, hello!
Hello! I'm Ted. Hello, hello, hello!
Hello, I'm Digger. Hello, hello, hello!
Hello, I'm Dot. Hello, hello, hello!

Hello! I'm Kelly. Hello, hello, hello!
Hello! I'm Pat. Hello, hello, hello!
Hello, I'm Kumi. Hello, hello, hello!

Hello, hello, hello!

Hello, I'm Joe. Hello, hello, hello!
Hello! I'm Jane. Hello, hello, hello!
Hello! I'm Chris. Hello, hello, hello!

Hello, hello, hello!

Unit 1

The Kangaroo Chant

Lion, lion, * * kangaroo
Lion, lion, * * kangaroo

Penguin, penguin, * * kangaroo
Penguin, penguin, * * kangaroo

Polar bear, polar bear, * kangaroo
Polar bear, polar bear, * kangaroo

Giraffe, giraffe, * * kangaroo
Giraffe, giraffe, * * kangaroo

Gorilla, gorilla, * * kangaroo
Gorilla, gorilla, * * kangaroo

Kangaroo, kangaroo, * kangaroo
Kangaroo, kangaroo, * kangaroo

The Zoo Song

What is it?
　　It's a penguin.
What is it?
　　It's a lion.
What is it?
　　It's a polar bear.
A penguin, a lion, a polar bear. *

What is it?
　　It's a giraffe.
What is it?
　　It's a gorilla.
What is it?
　　It's a kangaroo.
A giraffe, a gorilla, a kangaroo. *

I Can Jump

Jump, jump, I can jump.
　　Me, too.
Jump, jump, I can jump.
　　Me, too.
Jump, jump, I can jump.
　　Me, too.
Jump, jump, jump, jump,
　　I can jump!

Run, run, I can run.
　　Me, too.
Run, run, I can run.
　　Me, too.
Run, run, I can run.
　　Me, too.
Run, run, run, run, I can run!

Swim, swim, I can swim.
　　Me, too.
Swim, swim, I can swim.
　　Me, too.
Swim, swim, I can swim.
　　Me, too.
Swim, swim, swim, swim,
　　I can swim!

Stretch, stretch, I can stretch.
　　Me, too.
Stretch, stretch, I can stretch.
　　Me, too.
Stretch, stretch, I can stretch.
　　Me, too.
Stretch, stretch, stretch, stretch,
I can stretch!

Ant on the Apple

Ant on the apple, /a/, /a/, /a/.
Alligator, alligator, /a/, /a/, /a/.
Ant on the apple, /a/, /a/, /a/.
Sing the letter A.

Baby on the bus, /b/, /b/, /b/.
Butterfly, butterfly, /b/, /b/, /b/.
Baby on the bus, /b/, /b/, /b/.
Sing the letter B.

Unit 2

Long and Short

Long and short
Long and short
* * * *
Long and short

Big and small
Big and small
* * * *
Big and small

Fast and slow
Fast and slow
* * * *
Fast and slow

It's Long. It Isn't Short.

It's long. It isn't short.
It's big. It isn't small.
It's slow. It isn't fast.
It's long. It's big. It's slow.

It's short. It isn't long.
It's small. It isn't big.
It's fast. It isn't slow.
It's short. It's small. It's fast.

(Repeat)

Let's Look at the Turtle

Let's look at the turtle, the turtle,
the turtle.
Let's look at the turtle, the turtle.
　　Okay!

Let's feed the turtle, the turtle,
the turtle.
Let's feed the turtle, the turtle.
　　Okay!

Let's touch the starfish, the starfish,
the starfish.
Let's touch the starfish, the starfish.
　　Okay!

Let's hold the starfish, the starfish,
the starfish.
Let's hold the starfish, the starfish.
　　Okay!

Cake on the Car

Cake on the car, /c/, /c/, /c/.
Cat, cat, /c/, /c/, /c/.
Cake on the car, /c/, /c/, /c/.
Sing the letter C.

Dentist on the dinosaur, /d/, /d/, /d/.
Donut, donut, /d/, /d/, /d/.
Dentist on the dinosaur, /d/, /d/, /d/.
Sing the letter D.

Note: The symbol (*) that appears in some of the songs and chants represents handclaps.

The Occupations Chant

Doctor, doctor, * firefighter
Doctor, doctor, * firefighter
Doctor, doctor, * firefighter
Teacher * and student

Pilot, pilot, * firefighter
Pilot, pilot, * firefighter
Pilot, pilot, * firefighter
Teacher * and student

Vet, vet, * * firefighter
Vet, vet, * * firefighter
Vet, vet, * * firefighter
Teacher * and student

She's a Teacher!

She's a teacher! She's a teacher!
She's a teacher! She's a teacher!
(clap, clap, stomp, stomp, clap)

She's a pilot! She's a pilot!
She's a pilot! She's a pilot!
(clap, clap, stomp, stomp, clap)

She's a doctor! She's a doctor!
She's a doctor! She's a doctor!
(clap, clap, stomp, stomp, clap)

He's a vet! He's a vet!
He's a vet! He's a vet!
(clap, clap, stomp, stomp, clap)

He's a student! He's a student!
He's a student! He's a student!
(clap, clap, stomp, stomp, clap)

He's a firefighter! He's a firefighter!
He's a firefighter! He's a firefighter!
(clap, clap, stomp, stomp, clap)

Help the Teacher

Please...
Help the teacher.
Point to the teacher.
Help the teacher.
   * * Sure.
Help the teacher.
Point to the teacher.
Help.
Point.

Oh-oh-oh-oh, please...
Write the word.
Erase the word.
Write the word.

* * Sure.
Write the word.
Erase the word.
Write.
Erase.
Oh-oh-oh-oh-oh!

Elf on the Egg

Elf on the egg, /e/, /e/, /e/.
Elephant, elephant, /e/, /e/, /e/.
Elf on the egg, /e/, /e/, /e/.
Sing the letter E.

Farmer on the feather, /f/, /f/, /f/.
Fan, fan, /f/, /f/, /f/.
Farmer on the feather, /f/, /f/, /f/.
Sing the letter F.

Do You Like Cookies?

Do you like cookies? Yes, I do.
Do you like cookies? Yes, I do.
Do you like cookies? Yes, I do.
* * * Me, too!

Do you like burgers? Yes, I do.
Do you like burgers? Yes, I do.
Do you like burgers? Yes, I do.
* * * Me, too!

Do you like milk? Yes, I do.
Do you like milk? Yes, I do.
Do you like milk? Yes, I do.
* * * Me, too!

Do you like ice cream? Yes, I do.
Do you like ice cream? Yes, I do.
Do you like ice cream? Yes, I do.
* * * Me, too!

The Spaghetti Chant

Spaghetti, spaghetti, spaghetti-etti-etti!
Spaghetti, spaghetti, spaghetti-etti-etti!
   Juice, juice.
Spaghetti-etti-etti!
   Bread, bread.
Spaghetti-etti-etti!
   Salad, salad.
Spaghetti-etti-etti!
   Rice, rice.
Spaghetti-etti-etti!
   Pizza, pizza.

Spaghetti-etti-etti!
   Spaghetti, spaghetti.
Spaghetti-etti-etti!

I Want Pizza

I want pizza. Tra-la-la-la-la.
I want pizza. Tra-la-la-la-la.
I want bread.
I want juice.
I want salad.
I want rice.
I want pizza. Tra-la-la-la-la.

I want spaghetti. Tra-la-la-la-la.
I want spaghetti. Tra-la-la-la-la.
I want bread.
I want juice.
I want salad.
I want rice.
I want spaghetti. Tra-la-la-la-la.

Cut the Pizza

Cut the pizza, cut the pizza, please.
   * All right.
Eat the pizza, eat the pizza, please.
   * All right.

Pour the juice, pour the juice,
please.
   * All right.
Drink the juice, drink the juice,
please.
   * All right.

(Repeat)

Girl on the Goat

Girl on the goat, /g/, /g/, /g/.
Garden, garden, /g/, /g/, /g/.
Girl on the goat, /g/, /g/, /g/.
Sing the letter G.

Horse in the house, /h/, /h/, /h/.
Hen, hen, /h/, /h/, /h/.
Horse in the house, /h/, /h/, /h/.
Sing the letter H.

The Yo-Yo Chant

Yo-yo, puzzle! * * *
Yo-yo, ball! * * *
Yo-yo, jump rope! * * *
Yo-yo, doll! * * *
Yo-yo, kite! * * *
Yo-yo, ball! * * *

Yo-yo, jump rope! * * *
Yo-yo, doll! * * *

I Have a Ball

I have a ball. I have a ball.
I have a doll. I have a doll.
I have a jump rope.
I have a puzzle.
I have a yo-yo.
I have a kite.

I have a doll. I have a doll.
I have a ball. I have a ball.
I have a jump rope.
I have a puzzle.
I have a yo-yo.
I have a kite.

Watch Me

Watch me push the wagon.
   * Okay.
Watch me pull the wagon.
   * Okay.

Watch me push the wagon.
Watch me pull the wagon.
Watch me push the wagon.
   * Okay.

Watch me make the kite.
   * * Okay.
Watch me fly the kite.
   * * Okay.
Watch me make the kite. *
Watch me fly the kite. *
Watch me make the kite.
   * * Okay.

Ink on the Igloo

Ink on the igloo, /i/, /i/, /i/.
Insect, insect, /i/, /i/, /i.
Ink on the igloo, /i/, /i/, /i/.
Sing the letter I.

Jeans in the jar, /j/, /j/, /j/.
Jacket, jacket, /j/, /j/, /j/.
Jeans in the jar, /j/, /j/, /j/.
Sing the letter J.

Unit 6

The Clothing Chant

Shirt and sweater and
skirt and sweater and
dress and sweater and
cap. * *

(Repeat)

Shirt and jacket and
skirt and jacket and
dress and jacket and
cap. * *

(Repeat)

She Has a Shirt

She has a shirt. She has a shirt.
She has a shirt, oh yes! * *

She has a skirt. She has a skirt.
She has a skirt, oh yes! * *

He has a cap. He has a cap.
He has a cap, oh yes! * *

He has a jacket. He has a jacket.
He has a jacket, oh yes! * *

She has a dress. She has a dress.
She has a dress, oh yes! * *

He has a sweater. He has a sweater.
He has a sweater, oh yes! * *

Put on Your Cap

Put on your cap.
Quickly, quickly.

Take off your cap.
Quickly, quickly.

(Repeat)

Take out your sweater.
Quickly, quickly.
Put away your sweater.
Quickly, quickly.

(Repeat)

(Repeat all)

Ketchup on the Key

Ketchup on the key, /k/, /k/, /k/.
King, king, /k/, /k/, /k/.
Ketchup on the key,/k/, /k/, /k/.
Sing the letter K.

Lizard on the leaf, /l/, /l/, /l/.
Lemon, lemon, /l/, /l/, /l/.
Lizard on the leaf, /l/, /l/, /l/.
Sing the letter L.

Mouse on the moon, /m/, /m/, /m/.
Monkey, monkey, /m/, /m/, /m/.
Mouse on the moon, /m/, /m/, /m/.
Sing the letter M.

You Can Use my Hula Hoop

You can use my hula hoop.
   Really? Thank you! Really?
   Thank you! Really? Thank you!
You can use my hula hoop.
   Really? Thank you!
* * * You're welcome.

You can use my camera.
   Really? Thank you! Really?
   Thank you! Really? Thank you!
You can use my camera.
   Really? Thank you!
* * * You're welcome.

You can use my skateboard.
   Really? Thank you! Really?
   Thank you! Really? Thank you!
You can use my skateboard.
   Really? Thank you!
* * * You're welcome.

You can use my umbrella.
   Really? Thank you! Really?
   Thank you! Really? Thank you!
You can use my umbrella.
   Really? Thank you!
* * * You're welcome.

Unit 7

The Tick-Tock Chant

One o'clock, tick-tock
   One o'clock, tick-tock
Two o'clock, tick-tock
   Two o'clock, tick-tock
Three o'clock, tick-tock
   Three o'clock, tick-tock
Four o'clock, tick-tock
   Four o'clock, tick-tock

Five o'clock, tick-tock
   Five o'clock, tick-tock
Six o'clock, tick-tock
   Six o'clock, tick-tock
Seven o'clock, tick-tock
   Seven o'clock, tick-tock
Eight o'clock, tick-tock
   Eight o'clock, tick-tock

Nine o'clock, tick-tock
   Nine o'clock, tick-tock
Ten o'clock, tick-tock
   Ten o'clock, tick-tock

Eleven o'clock, tick-tock
    Eleven o'clock, tick-tock
Twelve o'clock, tick-tock
    Twelve o'clock, tick-tock

What Time Is It?

What time is it?
It's one o'clock.
Tick-tock. It's two o'clock. * *

What time is it?
It's three o'clock.
Tick-tock. It's four o'clock. * *

What time is it?
It's five o'clock.
Tick-tock. It's six o'clock. * *

What time is it?
It's seven o'clock.
Tick-tock. It's eight o'clock. * *

What time is it?
It's nine o'clock.
Tick-tock. It's ten o'clock. * *

What time is it?
It's eleven o'clock.
Tick-tock. It's twelve o'clock.*

Open the Door

Open the door slowly.
Close the door slowly.
Open the door slowly.
Close the door, door, door, door, door.
Open the door slowly.
Close the door slowly.
Open and close the door.* *

Pick up the clock slowly.
Put down the clock slowly.
Pick up the clock slowly.
Put down the clock, clock, clock, clock, clock.
Pick up the clock slowly.
Put down the clock slowly.
Pick up and put down the clock.**

Numbers in the Nest

Numbers in the nest, /n/, /n/, /n/.
Necklace, necklace, /n/, /n/, /n/.

Numbers in the nest, /n/, /n/, /n/.
Sing the letter N.

Ox in the office, /o/, /o/, /o/.

Octopus, octopus, /o/, /o/, /o/.
Ox in the office, /o/, /o/, /o/.
Sing the letter O.

Unit 8

The Seven-Day Chant

Sunday, Monday,
Tuesday, Wednesday,
Thursday, Friday,
* Saturday.

Sunday, Monday,
Tuesday, Wednesday,
Thursday, Friday,
* Saturday.

(Repeat)

What Day Is It?

Today is Sunday.
Today is Sunday.
Today is Sunday.
Tra-la-la-la-la-la.

Today is Monday.
Today is Monday.
Today is Monday.
Tra-la-la-la-la-la.

Today is Tuesday.
Today is Tuesday.
Today is Tuesday.
Tra-la-la-la-la-la.

Today is Wednesday.
Today is Wednesday.
Today is Wednesday.
Tra-la-la-la-la-la.

Today is Thursday.
Today is Thursday.
Today is Thursday.
Tra-la-la-la-la-la.

Today is Friday.
Today is Friday.
Today is Friday.
Tra-la-la-la-la-la.

Today is Saturday.
Today is Saturday.
Today is Saturday.
Tra-la-la-la-la-la.

Plant a Tree

Plant a tree, plant a tree.
Plant, plant, plant a tree with me.

Climb a tree, climb a tree.
Climb, climb, climb a tree with me.

Draw a picture, draw a picture.
Draw, draw, draw a picture with me.

Paint a picture, paint a picture.
Paint, paint, paint a picture with me.

(Repeat)

Puppy in the Popcorn

Puppy in the popcorn, /p/, /p/, /p/.
Parrot, parrot, /p/, /p/, /p/.
Puppy in the popcorn, /p/, /p/, /p/.
Sing the letter P.

Queen on the quilt, /q/, /q/, /q/.
Question mark, question mark,
/q/, /q/, /q/.
Queen on the quilt, /q/, /q/, /q/.
Sing the letter Q.

Unit 9

The Weather Chant

Hot, * * sunny *
    Hot, * * sunny *
Cold, * * sunny *
    Cold, * * sunny *
Hot, * * cloudy *
    Hot, * * cloudy *

Cold, * * cloudy *
    Cold, * * cloudy *
Hot, * * windy *
    Hot, * * windy *
Cold, * * windy *
    Cold, * * windy *
Hot, * * rainy *
    Hot, * * rainy *
Cold, * * rainy *
    Cold, * * rainy *

How's the Weather?

How's the weather?
    It's cloudy.
How's the weather?
    It's cold.
How's the weather?
    It's rainy.
How's the weather?
    It's hot.

How's the weather?
    It's sunny.
How's the weather?
    It's hot.

How's the weather?
   It's windy.
How's the weather?
   It's cold.

It's sunny.
It's rainy.
It's windy.
It's cold.

It's sunny.
It's cloudy.
It's windy.
It's hot.

Let's Get on the Train

Let's get on the train.
   * * All right.
Let's get off the train.
   * * All right.
Get on the train, get off the train.
* * * * * * *

Let's get in the car.
   * * All right.
Let's get out of the car.
   * * All right.
Get in the car, get out of the car.
* * * * * * * *

(Repeat)

Rooster on the Rainbow

Rooster on the rainbow, /r/, /r/, /r/.
Rabbit, rabbit, /r/, /r/, /r/.
Rooster on the rainbow, /r/, /r/, /r/.
Sing the letter R.

Seal in the sailboat, /s/, /s/, /s/.
Sun, sun, /s/, /s/, /s/.
Seal in the sailboat, /s/, /s/, /s/.
Sing the letter S.

Talk Time 3

Please Wash Your Face

Please wash your face!

We're late. We're late. Please wash
your face.
We're late. We're late. Please wash
your face.
We're late. We're late. Please wash
your face.
   Okay, Mom.

Please brush your teeth!

We're late. We're late. Please brush
your teeth.
We're late. We're late. Please brush
your teeth.
We're late. We're late. Please brush
your teeth.
   Okay, Mom.

Please get dressed!

We're late. We're late. Please get
dressed.
We're late. We're late. Please get
dressed.
We're late. We're late. Please get
dressed.
   Okay, Dad.

Please pack your bag!

We're late. We're late. Please pack
your bag.
We're late. We're late. Please pack
your bag.
We're late. We're late. Please pack
your bag.
   Okay, Dad.

Unit 10

Write Stories, Read Books

Stories * *
Write stories * *
Books * * *
Read books * * *
Pictures * *
Color pictures * *
Songs * * *
Sing songs * * *
Jumping jacks *
Do jumping jacks *
Hands * * *
Hold hands * *

(Repeat)

What We Do at School

We do jumping jacks at school.
* * * *
We do jumping jacks at school.
* * * *
We sing songs at school.
We read books at school.
We do jumping jacks at school.
* * * *

We color pictures at school.
* * * *

We color pictures at school.
* * * *
We hold hands at school.
We write stories at school.
We color pictures at school.
* * * *

Talk to Your Friend

Talk to your friend. Talk to your friend.
* * Please talk to your friend.
   Okay.

Listen to your friend. Listen to your
friend.
* * Please listen to your friend.
   Okay.

Raise your hand. Raise your hand.
* * Please raise your hand.
   Okay.

Put down your hand. Put down
your hand.
* Please put down your hand.
   Okay.

(Repeat)

Tiger on the Table

Tiger on the table, /t/, /t/, /t/.
Telephone, telephone, /t/, /t/, /t/.
Tiger on the table, /t/, /t/, /t/.
Sing the letter T.

Umbrella on the umpire, /u/, /u/, /u/.
Upside down, /u/, /u/, /u/.
Umbrella on the umpire, /u/, /u/, /u/.
Sing the letter U.

Unit 11

Play, Play

Play, play, play, play.
Play soccer, play, play, play.
Play cards, play, play, play.
Play basketball, play, play, play.
Play chess, play, play, play.

Play the violin. * * *
Play the piano. * * *
Play the violin. * * *
Play the piano. * * *

Play soccer, play, play, play.
Play cards, play, play, play.
Play basketball, play, play, play.
Play chess, play, play. * *

Yes, I Can

Can you play the violin?
    Yes, I can.
Can you play the violin?
    No, I can't.

Can you play basketball?
    Yes, I can.
Can you play basketball?
    No, I can't.

Can you play soccer?
    Yes, I can.
Can you play soccer?
    No, I can't.

Can you play chess?
    Yes, I can.
Can you play chess?
    No, I can't.

Can you play cards?
    Yes, I can.
Can you play cards?
    No, I can't.

Can you play the piano?
    Yes, I can.
Can you play the piano?
    No, I can't.

Yes, I can!

I Can Kick the Soccer Ball

I can kick the soccer ball,
the soccer ball, the soccer ball.
I can kick the soccer ball.
    * * * * Great!

I can bounce the basketball,
the basketball, the basketball.
I can bounce the basketball.
    * * * * Great!

I can throw the soccer ball,
the soccer ball, the soccer ball.
I can throw the soccer ball.
    * * * * Great!

I can catch the basketball,
the basketball, the basketball.
I can catch the basketball.
    * * * * Great!

Vase on the Violin

Vase on the violin, /v/, /v/, /v/.
Vest, vest, /v/, /v/, /v/.
Vase on the violin, /v/, /v/, /v/.
Sing the letter V.

Worm on the watermelon, /w/,
/w/, /w/.
Window, window, /w/, /w/, /w/.
Worm on the watermelon, /w/,
/w/, /w/.
Sing the letter W.

Unit 12

The Rooms Chant

Bathroom, bedroom, * living room
    Bathroom, bedroom, * living
room
Kitchen, bedroom, * living room
    Kitchen, bedroom, * living room
Yard, bedroom, * living room
    Yard, bedroom, * living room

Bedroom, bathroom, * dining room
    Bedroom, bathroom, * dining
room

Kitchen, bathroom, * dining room
    Kitchen, bathroom, * dining
room
Yard, bathroom, * dining room
    Yard, bathroom, * dining room

Where Are You?

Where are you?
    I'm in the living room.
Where are you?
    I'm in the kitchen.
Where are you?
    I'm in the dining room.
Where are you? * *

Where are you?
    I'm in the bathroom.
Where are you?
    I'm in the yard.
Where are you?
    I'm in the bedroom.
Where are you? * *

(Repeat)

Turn Off the Light

Turn on the light, please.
    All right.
Wash the dishes, please.
    All right.
Dry the dishes, please.
    All right.
Turn off the light, please.
    All right.

Turn on the light,
Wash the dishes,
Dry the dishes,
Turn off the light.

(Repeat)

Fox in the Box

Fox in the box, /x/, /x/, /x/.
Six, six, /x/, /x/, /x/.
Fox in the box, /x/, /x/, /x/.
Sing the letter X.

Yarn on the yo-yo, /y/, /y/, /y/.
Yellow, yellow, /y/, /y/, /y/.
Yarn on the yo-yo, /y/, /y/, /y/.
Sing the letter Y.

Zebra on the zipper, /z/, /z/, /z/.
Zero, zero, /z/, /z/, /z/.
Zebra on the zipper, /z/, /z/, /z/.
Sing the letter Z.

Talk Time 4

I'm Ready to Study English

I'm ready to study English!

I'm ready to study English.
I'm ready to study English.
    Good! Let's get started.
* Okay.

I'm ready to rake the leaves!

I'm ready to rake the leaves.
I'm ready to rake the leaves.
    Good! Let's get started.
* Okay.

I'm ready to bake cookies!

I'm ready to bake cookies.
I'm ready to bake cookies.
    Good! Let's get started.
* Okay.

I'm ready to clean the house!

I'm ready to clean the house.
I'm ready to clean the house.
    Good! Let's get started.
* Okay.

Word List

A

a	5
all right	22
alligator	7
ant	7
apple	7
are	61
at	10
away	30

B

baby	7
bake cookies	67
ball	24
basketball	56
bathroom	60
bedroom	60
big	8
books	52
bounce	58
box	63
bread	20
brush your teeth	51
burgers	19
bus	7
butterfly	7

C

cake	11
camera	35
can	6
can't	57
cap	28
car	11
cards	56
cat	11
catch	58
chess	56
clean the house	67
climb	42
clock	36
close	38
cloudy	44
cold	44
color pictures	52
cookies	19
cut	22

D

day	41
dentist	11
dining room	60
dinosaur	11
dishes	62
do jumping jacks	52
doctor	12
doll	24
donut	11
door	38
down	38
draw	42
dress	28
drink	22
dry	62

E

eat	22
egg	15
eight o'clock	36
elephant	15
eleven o'clock	36
elf	15
erase	14

F

fan	15
farmer	15
fast	8
feather	15
feed	10
firefighter	12
five o'clock	36
fly	26
four o'clock	36
fox	63
Friday	40
friend	54

G

garden	23
get dressed	51
get in	46
get off	46
get on	46
get out of	46
get started	66
giraffe	4
girl	23
goat	23
good	66
gorilla	4
great	58

H

hand	54
hands	52
has	29
have	25
he	29
he's	13
help	14
hen	23
hold hands	52
hold	10
horse	23
hot	44
house	23
how's	45
hula hoop	35

I

I	6
I'm	61
ice cream	19
igloo	27
in	46
ink	27
insect	27
is	5
isn't	9
it	5
it's	5

J

jacket	27
jar	27
jeans	27
juice	20
jump rope	24
jump	6
jumping jacks	52

K

kangaroo	4
ketchup	31
key	31
kick	58
king	31
kitchen	60
kite	24

L

leaf	31
lemon	31
let's	10
light	62
like	18
lion	4
listen to	54
living room	60
lizard	31
long	8
look at	10

M

make	26
me	6
milk	19
Monday	40
monkey	31
moon	31
mouse	31

N

necklace	39
nest	39
nine o'clock	36

no	57	put away	30	soccer	56	

no	57
numbers	39

O

o'clock	36
octopus	39
of	46
off	30
office	39
okay	10
on	30
one o'clock	36
open	38
out	30
ox	39

P

pack your bag	51
paint	42
parrot	43
penguin	4
piano	56
pick up	38
picture	42
pilot	12
pizza	20
plant	42
play	56
play basketball	56
play cards	56
play chess	56
play soccer	56
play the piano	56
play the violin	56
please	14, 50
point to	14
polar bear	4
popcorn	43
pour	22
pull	26
puppy	43
push	26

put away	30
put down	38
put on	30
puzzle	24

Q

queen	43
question mark	43
quickly	30
quilt	43

R

rabbit	47
rainbow	47
rainy	44
raise	54
rake the leaves	67
read books	52
ready	66
really	34
rice	20
room	60
rooster	47
run	6

S

sailboat	47
salad	20
Saturday	40
school	53
seal	47
seven o'clock	36
she	29
she's	13
shirt	28
short	8
sing songs	52
six o'clock	36
six	63
skateboard	35
skirt	28
slow	8
slowly	38
small	8

soccer	56
soccer ball	58
songs	52
spaghetti	20
starfish	10
stories	52
stretch	6
student	12
study English	67
sun	47
Sunday	40
sunny	44
sure	14
sweater	28
swim	6

T

table	55
take off	30
take out	30
talk	54
teacher	12
telephone	55
ten o'clock	36
thank you	34
the	10
three o'clock	36
throw	58
Thursday	40
tiger	55
time	37
today	41
to	14
too	6
touch	10
train	46
tree	42
Tuesday	40
turn off	62
turn on	62
turtle	10
twelve o'clock	36
two o'clock	36

U

umbrella	35, 55
umpire	55
up	38
upside down	55
use	34

V

vase	59
vest	59
vet	12
violin	56, 59

W

wash your face	51
watch	26
watermelon	59
we	53
we're	50
weather	45
Wednesday	40
what	5
where	61
window	59
windy	44
with	42
word	14
worm	59
write	14
write stories	52

Y

yard	60
yarn	63
yellow	63
yes	57
you	57
your	30
yo-yo	24, 63

Z

zebra	63
zero	63
zipper	63